T0098607

Streams of Income

# STREAMS OF INCOME

## RYAN REGER

NEW YORK

LONDON • NASHVILLE • MELBOURNE • VANCOUVER

# Streams of Income

## Living the Multiple Income Streams Dream

© 2019 Ryan Reger

All rights reserved. No portion of this book may be reproduced, stored in a retrieval system, or transmitted in any form or by any means—electronic, mechanical, photocopy, recording, scanning, or other—except for brief quotations in critical reviews or articles, without the prior written permission of the publisher.

Published in New York, New York, by Morgan James Publishing. Morgan James is a trademark of Morgan James, LLC. www.MorganJamesPublishing.com

ISBN 9781642792966 paperback
ISBN 9781642792973 eBook
Library of Congress Control Number: 2018911625

**Cover and Interior Design by:**
Chris Treccani
www.3dogcreative.net

Morgan James is a proud partner of Habitat for Humanity Peninsula and Greater Williamsburg. Partners in building since 2006.

Get involved today! Visit
MorganJamesPublishing.com/giving-back

Any monetary claims or examples in these materials are historical and do not indicate guarantees of future gains. Your level of success is dependent upon your unique situation, your devotion to your business, your skills, and your finances. The author and publisher shall in no event be held liable for any loss or other damages, including but not limited to special, incidental, or other damages. As with any business seek the advice of a competent legal, tax, and accounting or other professional. The author and publisher does not warrant the performance, effectiveness, or applicability of any websites in this book. All websites are for informational purposes only; they are not warranted for content, accuracy, or any other implied or explicit purpose.

For free companion videos and additional resources visit www.ryanreger.com/videos.

# DEDICATION

**This book is dedicated to:**

My wife, Melane, for the encouragement and
support to go after my dreams.

You, the reader, for you are why I wrote this
book.  You too can live your dreams.

# TABLE OF CONTENTS

# CHAPTER 1

# My Story

While this is not a biography about me, I do want to briefly share the story of the last few years of my life and how I got to where I am today.

Even though I know you want to hear about every detail of my life (kidding!), I'll start in 2004 when I read my first internet business book, *Silent Sales Machine*, by my now friend and mentor Jim Cockrum. At the time, I was living in Indiana and working for a congressman. I loved my job, but I knew I wanted to run my own business someday. I would always come up with business ideas but never really had the capital or the knowledge to implement them.

Fast forward to 2008 and I found myself without a job after the campaign I was managing was unsuccessful.

The only two things I knew at that time were:

1. I was moving to Texas
2. I was getting married

I had no idea what the next step in my career was.

I reached out to a couple of the local congressional offices and put my resume out on some of the online job sites, but nothing really excited me like the prospect of running my own business.

Back in 2005, my wife and mother-in-law started a small furniture business. They had access to some wholesale sources and started putting ads on craigslist for furniture. It was a nice little part-time income for them, but they really didn't have the time to make it a full-time enterprise. I didn't really know anything about furniture, but at the time it seemed like the easiest place to start since my wife and mother-in-law already had the contacts. It was my low-hanging fruit.

I was excited to get going, but my wife didn't believe that it could really be full-time income for us. She told me I needed to get a job and I agreed to continue looking while attempting to make the furniture business work.

So, I continued to submit my resume to online job sites, but my heart—and the majority of my time—went into building the furniture business. Instead of the one or two, here and there approach to posting craigslist ads, I ramped it up by posting several a day. The calls started coming in, and I continued posting.

It was slow at first, but we ended 2008 with $6,154 in sales.

In 2009, our momentum continued and by the grace of God we ended the year with a little over $250,000 in sales. And that was all through local Craigslist ads.

In those days, my wife and I literally did every part of the business ourselves. Her job was to post the ads and mine was all the heavy lifting: picking up the furniture at our supplier's warehouse and delivering it to our customers.

Now I can't even imagine driving all over the place doing deliveries, but the Lord gave me the grace to do it and I even enjoyed it.

Business was good until about May of 2012 when we noticed that our Craigslist ads were no longer working. In most of the areas we posted, the ads were taken down almost as soon as we put them up.

*This picture was taken in December 2011 at our old house. Our garage was full of furniture that was either to be delivered or picked up.*

We needed to do something different now that what we had always done was no longer producing results. The Lord knew what needed to happen and He already had the answer prepared in advance for us.

Jim Cockrum had recently written his book called *Free Marketing: 101 Low and No-Cost Ways to Grow Your Business, Online and Off* and had decided to auction off a signed copy of that book with all of the proceeds going to Hope Village, a ministry in Detroit, Michigan.

Because I was subscribed to Jim's newsletter, I was aware of the auction, but it wasn't until the final day of the auction that I knew I had to take action. I woke up that morning and saw an email that Jim had sent to subscribers announcing that it was the final day to place a bid.

I just knew that I had to win so I asked my wife if we could place a bid. She asked for how much and I told her. She was a little shocked but told me if that's what I thought we should do then do it.

I won. And the rest is history.

I say the rest is history because, since then, I have been fortunate enough to build a relationship with Jim Cockrum that has transformed my business. One of the added benefits of the auction was a 30-minute phone call with Jim. Since Jim lives about an hour from my parents' house in Indiana, I asked him if I could meet him for lunch one day in lieu of the phone call. He graciously agreed.

So, Melane and I planned a trip to Indiana to see my parents and to meet Jim. That was in September 2012.

*This picture was taken at our lunch with Jim Cockrum in Indianapolis. This was the first time we met him.*

That lunch changed our lives.

Jim gave us a lot of great ideas and tips, but the one we took action on right away was getting our furniture listed on Amazon. He also told us about Amazon's fulfillment program and encouraged us to find smaller items we could sell that way.

I'm honored to be able to call Jim a friend now and am blessed to have had the opportunity to be in his mastermind group and partner with him on numerous projects.

It's been over five years since we have sold a piece of furniture on craigslist. Remember, that used to be our *only* source of income.

Our business has changed so much that we don't even sell furniture anymore. In fact, my business has evolved a lot in even just the last year. At the time of this writing we have 16 different streams of income. Some of the streams include: Selling physical products on Amazon, Private Label Course/Coaching Program, Amazon Legends Program, Q4 Success Group, Live events, Book sales on Createspace and Kindle, Book sales on my own websites, Affiliate Marketing, and other courses and consulting jobs.

Since January of 2014 I have written three books related to selling online: *Real Wholesale Sources*, *Beyond Arbitrage*, and *Private Label the Easy Way*.

*Private Label the Easy Way* then became a course and mentoring program with over 2,300 students.

I never dreamed that I would write books or have a 2,300-plus-member group coaching program. And please know that I'm not sharing any of this to gloat. Far from that. I have no problem giving glory where glory is due. The Lord has been faithful and has brought opportunities across our path at the right time.

I'm sharing this to encourage you that if I can do it, you can too. I didn't start with 16 streams and neither will you. Get one going and watch how the opportunities come to take that one stream and branch it off into a new one.

I'll share more of my journey in the following chapters, but the intention of this book is not to tell you about me, but rather to paint a picture of how your life can look. I want to encourage you to dream again, to believe that you don't have to settle, that you don't have to live an ordinary, mundane life.

Your dreams can still come true.

I pray that this short book will be a blessing to you and help you see the opportunities all around you.

## CHAPTER 2

# Why I Wrote This Short Book

Back in 2009, I received a support letter from my cousin who was on her way to a short-term summer missions trip. As I started to read her letter, I began to weep because I so badly wanted to be able to fund the whole trip for her. I think she needed about $2,500.

Melane and I had just recently got married and our online business was in its infancy, so we were not in any position to give $2,500, but we did the best we could.

Since then, our business has grown and so has our income. If the Lord laid it on our hearts to give $2,500 for a short-term missions trip, we could. Don't get me wrong. I still consider $2,500 to be a good chunk of change, but because of what we have learned and implemented in our business, we're in a better position to meet needs like that.

What if every family had the extra income to be able to give to the causes they cared about or just to have some disposable income? Too many families are struggling, living paycheck to paycheck, and can't even think about being a blessing because they're just trying to pay the bills.

That is why I wrote this short book.

CHAPTER 3

# Three Online Business Models

There's no way I can teach you how to build an online business in just nine chapters, so I'm not even going to try.

I have invested thousands of dollars in my business education so it's unrealistic to expect you to learn what I've learned through this short book.

What I can do, though, is give you a very broad overview of the types of business models that exist online. Maybe one of these will jump out at you and help you get going in the right direction.

A lot of what I have learned about building an online business is from Jim Cockrum. In his book *Silent Sales Machine*, he outlines three broad categories of opportunities online:

1. Sell—Sell profitable, physical goods through your own site, Amazon, or eBay and find creative ways to automate the entire system and grow a huge customer following for future sales.

2. Expand—Find a profitable niche market, be a leader in that niche, and expand your influence by giving your followers fantastic content while also selling them products, services,

training, or information that is of interest to them.

3.  Consult—Help other business owners apply basic internet marketing skills to their business and prosper from your efforts in helping them succeed.

By the way, I HIGHLY recommend you get a copy of *Silent Sales Machine*. You can get it at www.ryanreger.com/ssm.

In the next three chapters, I will go into more detail on each one of these business models.

# CHAPTER 4

# Sell

This is the model I started with. As I mentioned in chapter one, we began selling furniture on Craigslist and then moved into eBay and Amazon.

There are dozens of ways to get started in the world of selling physical products online, including Amazon, eBay, Craigslist, and local Facebook groups. In my opinion, the best place to start is with Amazon.

Amazon is where everyone is already shopping, so why not go where the crowd is?

If I had to do it all over again, I would have started on Amazon much sooner. The furniture business was a God-send and I'm very thankful that when I got married I didn't have to go out and get a job. In fact, my wife and I have talked a lot about how grateful we are that I have never had to leave her from 8 AM to 6 PM like most husbands.

It's such a blessing to be able to own and operate a home business and be home with my wife and son at the same time. If we want to leave the house to go out to lunch and be gone for three hours, we have the option to do that. If I just don't feel like working one day, I don't have to call a boss and ask to take time off from work.

But, back to selling. When we were heavy into the furniture business, it was much more labor intensive. With Amazon, we can literally be in

Guatemala (where my sister-in-law and brother-in-law run an orphanage) and our business does not suffer. I just need an internet connection and I can go into my Amazon account and check to see what we've sold that day.

For anyone used to the eBay model of having to pack and ship everything on your own, you'll love Amazon's FBA (Fulfillment by Amazon) program.

The way this works is we (or our team that works for us) can send inventory we want to sell into Amazon's warehouses located around the country. Amazon will store that inventory for us and when a customer goes and places an order, the warehouse staff at Amazon will grab our item and ship it to the customer and send us the money.

FBA has revolutionized online selling.

So where do we get our inventory? Right now, we sell a lot of items that are our own brand

(Private Label) and from wholesale companies, but we didn't start there.

We got started by browsing a local thrift store and finding items that were selling for more on Amazon than what I could buy them for. It's not unheard of to buy an item for $2 or $3 and sell it for $20, $30, $40, or even $50 online. I've heard about sellers buying rare books at thrift stores and selling them for hundreds of dollars. While that might be a rare occurrence, it does happen.

Another source of inventory can be retail stores. We (or one of our team members) can go into a store like Walmart and find items that we can make a profit on. There are many sellers whose whole business is based on items they source at stores like Walmart and Target.

There are certain stores I used to dislike going into with my wife (one of them being fabric stores). However, now I'm eager to see what profitable inventory might be sitting on some shelf just waiting for me to grab. She'll go one way and I'll head straight to the clearance aisle to start seeing what I can find.

If you live in a remote area where maybe the closest Walmart is an hour away or if you're like my friend Jason from Singapore, you can still source products by going online. The same deals that you find in a store can often be found on a store's website. With this model, you also have the option to never even touch your inventory.

How is that possible?

Well, my friend Danny Stock has a fulfillment service in which you can have items shipped to their warehouse and they will prep it and ship it to Amazon for you. For more information about their service go to www.proprepandfulfillment.com.

That's what my friend Jason from Singapore does. He orders products online and has them shipped to a prep center, which sends them into Amazon for him.

Once you master sourcing inventory at retail stores, wholesale is the next step. Wholesale is buying items direct from the wholesaler and has some distinct advantages. One advantage is that you can constantly re-order the same item over and over again if it's selling well.

If you're interested in more information be sure to get my book *Beyond Arbitrage*.

The other source of inventory for us is private label and that is having your own brand of an item.

I've written a whole book about private label if you're interested in delving deeper into that subject.

Amazon is not the only game in town. eBay is a great option too. In fact, with Amazon's multi-channel fulfillment, you can sell something on eBay and have it shipped to your eBay customer from your Amazon inventory.

Like I said, this book is just meant to be an overview, so I couldn't possibly cover every marketplace you can sell on or present every idea for what you can sell.

Hopefully what I cover here will whet your appetite and help you decide which direction to go first.

For more information about selling on Amazon, I highly recommend the Proven Amazon Course (www.ryanreger.com/pac). In this course, you learn everything from how to open your account to how to get a private label project started.

CHAPTER 5

# Expand

This is a fun business model because you have the opportunity to be a blessing to others and teach them what you've learned.

Through my books, course, and my website I have had the privilege of teaching others some of what I have learned in building an online business.

It's humbling to read emails from people who have read one of my books, implemented the material, and have seen positive results like their husband being able to quit their job and be home with the family.

When I first got started building our business, I had no idea what niche I could be a leader in, but that question might be easier for you.

- What are your interests?
- What are you passionate about?
- What do you have a lot of knowledge about?

I guarantee you that there are many others out there with your same interests and you could be an influencer in that niche.

Take my friend Nancy Alexander for example.

Nancy makes beautiful wreaths and her business was selling them on eBay. After implementing the advice given to her by my mentor Jim Cockrum, she started teaching others how to make and sell wreaths.

She now has a large email list of people who look to her for the latest craft-making tips and strategies. She has written several books and even does coaching on how to create a craft business all under her overarching brand, Ladybug Wreaths.

Whatever your niche is, there is a group of hungry people waiting for your content and they will pay you for it.

Like I said, at first, I had no idea what knowledge I had that people would actually take out their credit card and send me money for, but as our business grew, so did my experience.

My first book, *Real Wholesale Sources*, came about because I found a bunch of wholesale sources where accounts could be created online and items shipped to my home. I figured other sellers would be interested in this, so I published a short book listing the sources with links.

That book came out at the beginning of 2013 and four years later, I still make money every single week from sales either on my website or through Amazon.

Then in 2014 my friend John Bullard Sr approached me about partnering to write a book about wholesale sourcing and we called it *Beyond Arbitrage*.

Then again in 2015 I launched *Private Label the Easy Way* because I found a method of sourcing private label products with very low risk and with a very small investment.

In April of 2015 I partnered with my friend Jenni Hunt to take *Private Label the Easy Way* and turn it into a course with group mentoring; thus, our Private Label the Easy Way mentoring program was launched. We started with around 30 students and we now have over 2,300 in just a three year period.

The biggest reason for such a sharp increase is that we partnered with my friend Jim

Cockrum and he promoted it to his large list of loyal followers. This absolutely would not have happened had I not built a relationship with him.

(I'll talk more about relationships later because they are so vital and have been a major factor in my success.)

My Private Label mentoring program has become a large stream of income for us but what's really cool is that several smaller streams have branched off from that main stream.

One of my favorite ways to serve my students is doing live events. There's nothing quite like the personal interaction and getting to know my students face-to-face. At the time of this writing, I just hosted a live event with two of my team members close to my home at the Gaylord Texan, a resort hotel in the Dallas-Fort Worth area. We had over 40 people fly from all over the country to attend this two-day event.

My first event didn't draw 40 people, but it was still a success.

Last year, I decided to host an event at my home and invite students from my mentoring program and people who are on my email list. You might wonder why I would ever invite strangers to my house. Well, I don't consider my students strangers, but the main reason I chose to have it at my home was that I had no idea if anyone would come so no one would know if that did happen.

I was pleased to have seven of my students come from all over the country at $897 each, which is not a bad pay day for a dinner the evening before and a full day of training the next day.

Another stream that has branched off is smaller mastermind groups. My partner, Jenni, and I created these eight-person groups that we join on a six-week journey with one call per week where we spend time talking about their business and how we can help them reach their private label goals. These are a lot of fun as we get to interact via a video conference and put faces with names.

Other various streams that have resulted from launching the mentoring program are webinars, promoting other people's products that are relevant to private label (affiliate marketing), and a membership site stocked full of vetted private label product ideas and suppliers.

The challenge now is that the opportunities are endless, and we have to pick and choose what will best serve our audience.

In all of the aforementioned cases, the knowledge that I gained through selling physical products on Amazon turned into other streams of income by sharing that knowledge.

Is there a strategy that you have used to grow a business or a tip that makes something easier? Or just anything that you have learned that is valuable information?

Someone is willing to pay you for that knowledge.

An objection I often hear from people about writing a book or creating a course is "There is already so much information out there about that topic."

That may be true, but there is nothing on that subject from your viewpoint or from your experience until you create it.

There is a plethora of information about how to build a business selling products online, but let's say that your story is that you didn't start until you were 70 years old and now, five years later, you're making more from your online business than you ever did in your 40 years of working at your old job.

Do you think there is anyone else who would be interested in hearing about how you did that?

You bet there is. And guess what?

Many people in your same age bracket have money to spend on courses and coaching. Do you think they'd rather learn from someone who is 30 years younger or from someone they strongly identify with?

You got it. They are going to be more drawn to someone they strongly identify with, especially if they have a similar background.

For me personally, there is no feeling quite like hearing someone tell me their husband was able to quit his job to be home with his family because of what they learned from me. It's very humbling. And to be able to share knowledge to help someone else and be paid for it is an amazing feeling. The success stories make me happy. The money makes my wife happy (kidding!).

In all seriousness, it's very rewarding to have the privilege of helping others succeed. If you have a desire to explore how you can monetize your knowledge and experience, please check out the Master Plan of Influence program I co-created with my friend Jenni Hunt.

We have noticed a pattern in how we took a book and expounded on it and then created multiple streams from one starting point. This exact method can be used in almost any field and we'd love to help you take your knowledge and get it into a book, course, coaching program, etc.

Go to www.masterplanofinfluence.com for more information.

# CHAPTER 6

# Consult

You might be thinking "How in the world would I ever be a consultant when I'm not an expert at anything?"

Good question.

The truth is that you are an expert at something, but the secret of consulting is that you don't have to know everything.

You just need to partner with people that have the knowledge that you don't.

Let's say that you want to start a business helping to create and improve websites for local businesses. To start such a business, you might think that you have to know how to create a beautiful website from scratch, but all you would really need is the ability to get new customers. For not very expensive, you could hire out every bit of technical work needed to create a nice website.

If you have a desire to help people, then consulting is very rewarding. Have you ever walked into a business and wondered how much longer they would be open because of their lack of customers?

Here's a portion of one of my blog posts from 2014 that explains how there are businesses in your local area that need you.

---

"I had the tremendous opportunity to speak at a small internet marketing conference in Denver this past week. My wife was able to come with me and we took some time to sightsee.

We were doing some shopping and walked into a small shop that specializes in antique maps and high-end gifts. The manager was very friendly and began to chat with us about the store. She told us about the different maps and historical pieces she had.

As a history buff it was fascinating, but the whole time I was thinking "Are they selling online?" and "How can I help them?" I can't shut it off. :) When I meet someone, I'm thinking "Is there a way for me to help them with their business or to start a business?"

Melane and I have been so blessed to be able to work together and have not had to have "real jobs" during our whole marriage. We want others to be able to experience the same blessings.

So, we asked that store manager if they were selling online and she said they were working on their website, but it was not live yet. When we told her that many of the items in the store could be sold on Amazon, she was amazed since she thought Amazon was just for books. She knew eBay might be a fit for the one of a kind items but had not tried it yet.

We told her about our business and about how we use Amazon's fulfillment service (FBA). She looked at us like we were online selling geniuses. I left my business card and told her I would be happy to help her get started online.

Even if you've only been selling online for a few months, you have a tremendous amount of knowledge and can benefit businesses around you and get paid well for it. Trust me when I say that you know more than you think you do. Offline businesses need your expertise and you can benefit financially as a result.

I don't consider myself an expert in striking up conversations, but all we did was ask questions about her store, and it led to telling her about our business. She was intrigued and began asking us how that all worked. It may or may not lead to a business opportunity for us, but it was easy and I'm sure going to be on the lookout for more opportunities to help offline businesses get started online.

So, I encourage you to take what you know and use that as an opportunity to benefit others. There is gold in your own backyard."

---

We did not end up working with this store, but there are opportunities like this everywhere. How many businesses in your local area don't even have a Facebook page?

A whole business model could be assisting local businesses to take advantage of Facebook. I know one business owner who is paying $500 per month to have someone update their Facebook page every day and engage with customers.

Your idea of fulfilling work might not be spending all day on Facebook, but I guarantee you could outsource the actual work and spend your time getting new customers.

An example in our business of the C model (Consult) is a partnership with my alma mater Huntington University in Huntington, Indiana. I saw an article that was shared by one of Huntington's professors about how the business department had created a unique for-profit business of providing services like accounting to local companies.

Very soon after, I reached out to that professor, updated her on what I had been doing, and asked if the university would entertain the idea of starting an Amazon business selling physical products. A few phone calls later and I was on a plane back to Indiana to set it all up with them under a consulting arrangement in which I get a percentage of their monthly profits.

Now business students at Huntington have the opportunity to work in a real-life business and get hands-on training. How much more valuable is that than relying on what they learn in a book or in class?

There are millions of opportunities out there like this. You just have to open up your eyes to see them. If you're interested in more information about this business model, I highly recommend the Proven Business Consulting Course (www.ryanreger.com/pbc), a site with all kinds of information and resources related to building this type of business.

## CHAPTER 7

# Six Little Bullet Points

During my morning quiet time back in January 2009, I wrote these six little bullet points in my journal under the heading "My Dream Position":

- Flexible Hours
- High Pay
- Work from Home
- Vacation time whenever I need it
- Great people to work with

- A cause, mission, and vision I love and am passionate about

In January 2009, our furniture business was still in its infancy. I had no idea at the time whether or not it was going to work. So, I was still checking out job websites and exploring other options. My dream was to be in business for myself, but I also had to make sure I could take care of my wife.

Fast-forward to 2018 and I've been living this dream for several years now. I never had to go get a "real job" and our business has expanded every year since. It doesn't look anything like it did back in 2009. Selling furniture is a thing of the past and I'm making more money and working much less. I'm not quite at the four-hour work week, but I really can work as much or as little as I want to.

My wife and I just had our first child last year and I can't tell you how thankful I am to be able to be home and experience every single moment of his little life. My work fits into my lifestyle, not the other way around, which is the case for most people.

My wife hasn't done anything in our business for over two years and has been able to focus on the most important job: being mom. None of this would be possible without the multiple streams of income we built over the years.

- *Can you imagine waking up without an alarm clock?*
- *Can you imagine not having to fight traffic to go to a job you don't even like?*
- *Can you imagine having the freedom and the finances to take a trip with your family whenever you want to?*
- *Can you imagine not stressing when you have an unexpected bill?*

- *Can you imagine being able to give more to your church or to your favorite charity?*
- *Can you imagine loving your work?*

You don't have to imagine all of this. It can be your reality, but you must believe that it's possible and you must have a plan to get there. I hope that this short little book will help you believe in yourself again and see that it is possible to live your dreams. And it's my prayer that one of these business models can help you get there.

What are your six bullet points? Maybe you have eight or 10 or just four. It doesn't matter. **Write them down**.

In my opinion, this step cannot be overlooked. No matter what business model you choose, I believe you have to have a vision.

Give yourself permission to dream again.

Here are some questions I want you to take some time to think about and then write your answers down somewhere.

- *What does your ideal day look like?*
- *Where do you want to be five years from now?*
- *What is your motivation to make the above happen?*

I love the question "What does your ideal day look like?" Be as detailed as you want in answering this. Six years ago, I wrote down my answers to this question and today all five dreams are reality and back then I had no idea how I would achieve them, but I did. There is something about writing down your dreams that is powerful.

Now I love vision boards because it allows me to see my dreams. You could have an actual bulletin board where you pin pictures that represent what you desire, or you could be like me and just create a collage on your computer with pictures. It doesn't matter. The important thing is that you look at it often to remind yourself of what you're working for.

The third question, "What is your motivation for making the above happen," is also called your "Why?". Why do you want to start a business?

Many think the answer to that question is to make money, but I don't believe that money is really a good motivator. It's what money can do for you that is the true motivator.

- Do you want to be able to quit your job so that you can spend more time with your family?
- Do you want to have the freedom to travel anywhere at any time?
- Do you want to pay off all your debt?

- Do you want to not have to live paycheck to paycheck?
- Do you want to be able to give more?

Money is a tool that will help you achieve all of these things. Are you ever going to be able to do any of this with your current situation? If not, change your situation.

It's never too late to start. We live in the greatest time to be an entrepreneur. There is so much opportunity. You just have to take action.

CHAPTER 8

# Secrets of My Success

## Build Relationships

I can emphatically say that my life and my business would not be as successful as it is today without the relationships I've built.

It might seem like a stretch to say that my lunch with Jim Cockrum back in 2012 changed my life, but it's true. Because of what I've learned from him and the projects we've partnered on, my business has grown exponentially.

Because of meeting Jenni Hunt back in 2014 at a conference, we now have the enormous privilege and responsibility of 2,300 plus students in our private label mentoring program.

In 2012 I was asked to be part of a mastermind group with seven other guys who are Amazon sellers. We named ourselves MM8 for Mastermind 8. These guys are some of my best friends and business partners and I know that my business would not be as successful had I not met them.

The point is: don't get stuck behind your computer thinking you can do all of this by yourself. Get out and go to conferences or find a local Meetup group. Whatever you have to do to network with people in your same business I promise will pay you big dividends.

## Focus

In my business this can be very challenging because every day there is a new course or offer that promises this or that. We call these things "Shiny Objects." They may be great information and worth every penny, but it's not worth taking your focus off of what you're currently building.

I've been doing this long enough to see that these offers will come around again. Resist the temptation to bounce around from one idea to the next. Get one business or stream going. Then and only then should you start a new stream of income.

I wrote a blog post about this topic recently. You can find it at www.ryanreger.com/possible-work-less-make/.

**Pray as though everything depended on God. Work as though everything depended on you.**

This quote is from Saint Augustine who lived in the first century, but it's timeless.

It's okay if you don't believe the same way I do. We can still be friends but permit me to tell you that there is no way to explain some of the amazing favor I have had in my life and business.

It's by the grace of God that when I moved to Texas my wife and mother-in-law already had a business that I could plug into and turn into (with work) a full-time business.

It's by the grace of God that I happened to win that auction back in 2012 and start a relationship with my friend and mentor that has created income for both of us and numerous success stories for our students.

It's by the grace of God that I happened to meet Jenni Hunt at a conference in 2014 and start a relationship that has turned into multiple streams of income for each of us (again with lots of work on our part).

It's by the grace of God and all the work we have put into our business that now my wife and I can be at home to enjoy raising our little boy and not miss a single moment.

I could go on and on, but you get it. God has blessed us and it's truly an honor to have our ministry (yes, I believe my work is my ministry) of helping others achieve their dreams.

# CHAPTER 9

# Final Thoughts

I sincerely hope that this short book has encouraged you to see the possibilities right before you. You can live your dreams and building an online business may be the vehicle to get you there.

It's your turn to take action.

Which of the models seem to fit you the best?

As you enter the online business world, you'll soon see a million different self-proclaimed gurus peddling course after course promising you quick riches. Resist the urge to go after these shiny objects.

None of the business models I referenced are a quick way to get rich. I don't believe there is a quick method to get rich online. At least not anything that is legal. Every single one of my friends that make their full-time income online didn't get there overnight. Neither did my wife and I.

But you can get there, and I hope I have encouraged you to get started. You may just want to supplement your income and that's fine, but if you are looking to go at this full-time then please know that is also possible.

If you're serious about taking the next steps, please check out the resources page for my suggested resources that can help you get started.

I sincerely hope that this book has been valuable to you and has at least given you an idea about what you can do to build your own online business.

P.S. I'd like to stay in touch with you. Please go to www.ryanreger.com and fill out your name and email to get updates. Also feel free to connect with me on Facebook at www.facebook.com/ryanreger/. For free companion videos and additional resources visit www.ryanreger.com/videos.

# RESOURCES

Proven Amazon Course (www.ryanreger.com/pac): By Jim Cockrum and expert contributors; Described as the most comprehensive, selling on Amazon.com course in the world and the largest expert-monitored Amazon selling discussion forum in the world.

Private Label Mentoring Program (www.provenprivatelabel.com): Let me help you launch your own private label product on Amazon with very little risk and a minimal investment.

Jim Cockrum Coaching (www.ryanreger.com/jim-cockrum-coaching): The best internet marketing coaching program on the market.

MySilentTeam Facebook Group (www.ryanreger.com/mst): Facebook group hosted by Jim Cockrum and his team of expert moderators. You don't have to build your business alone. This Facebook group is a great place to get questions answered and meet other entrepreneurs.

Master Plan of Influence (www.masterplanofinfluence.com): The Master Plan of Influence (MPI) is a simple strategy that virtually anyone can use to increase or amplify their message. We have applied it over and over again—and it works! If you have something to teach or a message that serves to help others, this may just be the plan for you!

# ABOUT THE AUTHOR

By God's grace Ryan has built a thriving online business with multiple streams of income ranging from selling physical products to a variety of books and courses on the topic of starting and growing an  online business. Ryan's passion is to help people discover their gifts and talents and use them to fulfill their purpose in life – thus the reason for this book.

Ryan is happily married to his wife, Melane, and is a proud father to his son, Callen. They reside in Southlake, TX.

Check out Ryan's website ryanreger.com for more information and resources.

Printed in the USA
CPSIA information can be obtained
at www.ICGtesting.com
JSHW072029140824
68134JS00045B/3851